LONG STORY SHORT

i survived

NISHI

Made with ❤ on the Notion Press Platform

www.notionpress.com

CONTENTS

For everyone who is coping with their tortured hearts, I see you and understand you all too well

ACKNOWLEDGMENTS

With heartfelt gratitude, I extend my thanks to Notion-Press Publishing for helping me turn my dream into a reality.

To my incredible parents, thank you for always believing in me and pushing me to chase my dreams. Your love and encouragement have been my guiding light.

Ferb, your constructive criticism has helped me grow as a writer in ways I never thought possible. I am grateful for your honest feedback.

To my dear girls—Akshu, Shristi, and Maitraiyi—you have been my source of inspiration and strength. Your unwavering support has meant the world to me. When you hype me up, it makes my heart swell. You guys are my Taylor Swift songs.

Sarrah and Nonu, your friendship has been a constant source of comfort and encouragement. Thank you for always being there for me.

To all my friends, thank you for encouraging and cheering on me. Though I cannot name each one of you, I am still endlessly grateful.

To my family, I am delighted to have your love and support.

And to every person who picked up my book, I am beyond grateful. I hope you enjoy the journey within these pages.

With Love.
Nishi

PLAYLIST

Long Story Short – **Taylor Swift**

Fine Line – **Harry Styles**

Family Line – **Conan Gray**

Mess It Up – **Gracie Abrams**

Chemtrails Over The Country Club – **Lana Del Rey**

Clean (Taylor's Version) – **Taylor Swift**

End Of Beginning – **DJO**

Watch – **Billie Eilish**

PHASES – **Chase Atlantic**

Die For You – **The Weeknd**

Nobody – **Mitski**

The Story Never Ends – **Lauv**

They Don't Make 'Em Like You Anymore – **Lany**

18 – **One Direction**

Who Says – **Selena Gomez And The Scene**

Who's Afraid of Little Old Me? – **Taylor Swift**

I Found – **Amber Run**

The Manuscript – **Taylor Swift**

People Watching – **Conan Gray**

The Albatross – **Taylor Swift**

Can't Catch Me Now – **Olivia Rodrigo**

I Can Do It With a Broken Heart – **Taylor Swift**

ODES FROM THE
MORNING SUN

she heals a heart she didn't break

people can't see a woman peak in her career

so all they do is spread hate

they judge her on what she wears

at this point i love that she doesn't care

her music can make you cry

and you won't stop until your tears dry

you can dance to her melody

'cause she left a real freaking legacy

she taught me that love is golden,

and you can't fix everything that's broken

and maybe some things will never be spoken.

her lyrics give away so much into folklore

she will be known forevermore

-    *a swiftie*

in a world full of unsafe men

you're the only one who makes me feel safe over and over again

-       *my dad*

i'm the worst friend you'll have

i'm selfish because i'm never there

i don't pick up your calls or answer your texts

maybe there's more going on than just despair

im up every night

but i don't scroll or share

it's my heavy breaths and a blanket i hold tight

i feel guilty for not being there for you but wanting for you to care

im trying to change it

because you mean so much to me than you'll ever know

my efforts might look like shit

'cause i know i failed to show

slumped and defeated

was my heart once,

she patted my back and

picked me up.

-    *best friend*

when i was a baby,

you lifted me up on your shoulder.

when i recall all of my childhood memories

i see yours and mom's faces, giggling & laughing

and i feel like a flower that never had to worry

you watered me, i bloomed gleefully like the spring

home isn't the same without you

it misses its warmth, becoming colder

'i love you' i don't say it much

but i do, especially now that im growing older

i wanna cherish all of our souvenirs

for, they will always be with me forevermore

-    *the favorite child*

she is a folklore girlie

who wakes up too early

she loves reading

books about characters who love sneaking

she's got these enchanting brown eyes

a freaking angel in disguise

she's got the most amazing smile

also a real good style

she is a girl no one can even imagine in their wildest dreams

when she laughs her face beams

her voice is very comforting

like flowers blooming in spring

she deserves to be written about forever

'cause she's a one-of-a-kind treasure

she's an exquisite poem as well as a poetess

a lover girl full of happiness

- *my favorite tortured poet.*

i hold so much power within

using it could be consequential

would i win or would i be committing a sin

there was no godmother to guide

nobody to have ever tried

they were too scared of me to

ever stand beside

they say i'm not normal

and some say i'm lethal

but i'm only fighting my internal battle

my magic lies inside me

but nobody can see

so i fight 'cause i wanna be free

- *a favorite character*

it's been a while since we shared a few laughs

i catch us laughing everyday but through our old photographs

some days i feel like its okay even if we're not friends
anymore

i half-heartedly try to convince myself that our friendship
wasn't meant for evermore

some days i miss you like the flowers miss the rain

so i check your account to see you happy and it numbs my pain

i wish we could be friends again

but a part of me doesn't want to end up in the same old chain

do you miss how we used to go out to eat?

or how in the evenings, we used to walk down the street?

did you notice how our deep talks on the terrace

changed into gazing into the dark night lacking stars?

did you notice how the yellows and pinks of our friendship
turned to sad greys and black colors?

funny how it all ended a little too soon

i still long for those crazy afternoons in june

this a letter for my ex best friend,

i'm sorry we couldn't be a part of each other's life until the
end.

i fell into your arms

you gave me your home

it was too much to ask but

i never would've survived on my own.

- *a book reference*

i need you for keeps

from the moment we met

you told me you were like a river

something that i'd never want to forget.

- *a book reference*

she is pretty like the sunflower

she is the one with a golden heart

she is the one who loves water

she is an absolute work of art

cute curly hair and joyous eyes

a face with the most glorious smiles

guess her favorite time of the year?

it's always the season of snow

write a book about her

it would be called – *"yellow"*

wish i had known three years back

i would be having my own girls gang

once lost faith in female friendship

cause i drowned in that sailing ship too quick

lost someone close

but won them when i lost all hopes

they're my *Sunflower, Magnolia* and *Aven*

we're a bouquet marvelously woven

with her, a little unhinged and quirky, is the conversation

my *Sunflower* has endless compassion

she's a workaholic and ambitious girl

my *Magnolia* is a lovergirl

she's a poet and an amazing writer

my *Aven* has always been an amazing fighter

these girls have become my chosen sisters

empathetic and the best listeners.

they hold my heart in their hand

i'll always be their number one fan

we're the type of flowers that people keep

under their pillows even while they sleep

a night we would remember all too well

how we danced around and screamed our hearts out

how we were clueless like our last few brain cells

one of our memorable hangout

we missed a few

but maybe they missed us too

vibing on the music with no care of the world

until our throats hurt and feet burned

- *concert tales*

26

SUNLIT MUSINGS

home never felt like home

maybe because my home lies in the lyrics of a poem

between the ink stained papers

among verses and its words

i love decembers.

you know why?

december feels like saying goodbyes.

it's like the end of a journey

but more to hope for.

it's christmas season, so there's that.

december is cozy

'cause you can go at your pace,

in your own mindset

about how you wanna do your next year.

december feels more homey

than any other month.

december feels like excitement.

it feels like promises.

december is chilly but it feels warm

like a blankie wrapped around you,

making everything better.

got a book of white sheets

stained them with coloured streaks

as the green turn into auburn leaves

there was a time

when i could write poetry effortlessly

and my fingers

understood my heart, oh, so easily

but now, my heart aches

makes me hate

but for the words to flow

all i can do is wait

what happens when we die?

do we sleep forever or fly through the sky?

do the birds sing or do they sob?

is it all clear or is it just a hazy fog?

do the poets write about us in heaven?

do we come back to life to go through hell again?

do we remember the people we left?

are we forgotten just as soon maybe for the best?

i believe in afterlife

so maybe heaven exists and so does hell

the devil burns them with a knife

and the angels shower us with what, nobody lives to tell

writing has always been her therapy

and if you had cared enough to see

her words reflected her internal beauty

as she weaved her enchanting story

i fell in love with the golden hour,

with the cold breeze that swayed my hair

with the mesmerizing long drives in the car

with the way, the sky made me feel so bare

books, i've found, are a way to save

pieces of yourself, until you are sleeping under the grave

books are my intoxicating narcotics

healing my heart in a way i never thought could fix

books are my home

the kind of place where i feel known; never alone

you are beautiful

some beauties are meant to be seen from afar

but a beauty like you is as precious as a star

you leave not a temporary mark but a permanent scar.

sometimes you want to fly

and rocket up so high

just to be immortal and never die

don't wanna hide and cry

don't wanna fake try

don't wanna pretend and lie

but all these dreams… *sigh*

what is poetry;

if not covering a white canvas in colorful shades

as enigmatic to understand as depths of the lakes

but don't you hate the immortality of fiction

or how we will not stop ageing, such a contradiction

TWILIGHT LOVE

"i love you," i ache to hear,

admit the truth, dispel the fear.

what lingers in your guarded soul?

is it real, the love you stole?

so, speak the truth, set me free,

break the chains of uncertainty.

-    *cry from a heartbroken lover*

my name on your lips

my body on your hips

that's when all of it clicks.

sweet whispers fill the air

thoughts of this ending isn't fair

'cause it's too painful to bear.

but they say all good things come to an end

and we can't always pretend.

we'll have to say goodbyes

with hurting moist eyes

and feed ourselves lies.

the men in my books always became better

but you left me standing only with a letter

the story of us ended before it even had a forever.

your crystal gaze was enough for my heart to thunder

was it butterflies of love or just my terrified nerves, i wonder?

-    *someone with a broken heart and trust issues*

your once warm sweater

now feels cold

it lost its warmth

maybe its story will always remain untold

i knew it all too well

when you painted my world with your fiery hell

all you did was yell

but all those warnings from others did foretell

you told me you adored my breathtaking smile

made me believe we'd never go out of style

oh,so subtly your words turned vile

leading to your unsolicited exile

you didn't like the mad woman

you had once seen

scary was the mess that you made

that was left for me to clean

i once thought love was maroon

like the wine you splashed across the room

leaving you for good on that 13th of june

gentle rain cleansed my heart that monsoon

and then we were done

thought too much until the next morn's sun

realized i never wanted to return

for, i didn't want myself to burn

the bruises that you gave me

not one, not two, but three

turned yellow soon and it hurt to see

you looked too glad to be separated from me

your cold emerald eyes gloomed

the sunflowers of our love never once bloomed

one day you'll be sobbing with my picture in your room

and i'll be the one you think about whenever you watch
the moon

but now are there still beautiful things?

where all of my invisible strings?

will i even have my marvelous happy endings?

but nonetheless, cheers to new beginnings

although i was your first everything

left you 'cause your love-bombing had my heart
bleeding

wrapped in your jacket's blissful embrace

for, it was a habit, i could never replace

the cold crystals drizzling didn't pause

you made us hot chocolate shrugging, 'just because'

the tv kept playing in the distance

you weaved our hands together in that instance

we danced to 'daylight' by taylor swift and harry styles

until we were a mess of giggles and smiles

i whispered, "you make me feel safe"

you smiled before leaning to caress my face,

"would you believe me if i said im falling in love?"

"i do believe that you and i are like doves",

i said softly, as the clock ticked above.

it was pretty late but one look at me & you knew

went out on the snow-covered porch,

only to lie flat on the cold soft snow beside you

and we left behind two ethereal snow angels

i felt it in my bones, we could never go back to being
strangers

the movie kept playing

your fingers in my hair kept twirling

my face nuzzling in the crook of your neck

lips still tingled from that little peck.

locked eyes; they gave it all away

my chestnut browns made out with your hazel gray

oh how yours were shining in delight

and mine reflected them; just as bright.

the peace around us felt strange

for it had never been such on my page

my book had always been messy

hence the serenity of our us felt different already

do no doubt my love for you

you are the sun, the moon, and star to my sky so blue

your hand in mine makes me believe

that you need me just as i need you for keeps

oh how long did i get lost in the thoughts?

i adored all the freckles on your face looking like tiny
hearts and dots

the way your soft lips tip up on the right side more

or how the little scar on your wrist looked like the sea
brushing the edge of a shore

how long did we sit gazing at each other

did you fall in love with me like i fell for you all over?

your eyes scream a joyous yes

while this dream seems a faraway haze nonetheless

we've not met

you don't know me and i don't know you yet

but this feeling inside of me screams that im going to
know you when i see

and maybe you'll feel the tug in your heart like you once
knew me

maybe you'll ask if you could buy me a drink

and i'll be so surprised; i'll only look at you and blink

i would tell you "no thanks, i can buy myself one"

you'll only laugh and ask "then shall we buy some?"

i would want to make it harder for you

but deep down you put me at ease that would be true

maybe we'll go on a date or few

and slowly and ridiculously i'll be falling for you

i won't tell you the truth though

for, i've been hurt before and people just go

i will be scared

i hope you will be prepared

maybe you'll gradually earn my trust

and learn all about how my cheeks blush

i know you don't understand what im trying to say

we've never met but i think about you everyday

my dear future lover this one is for you

i believe that you'll not be just a mark but a permanent
tattoo

my love was like autumn leaves

i fell for you like those shades of orange and yellows
from the trees

they say, oh to be loved by a writer,

and lord, isn't that true?

how many of your smiles had i written about in my
notes, only if you knew

my words never did justice to your beauty

i had never known that even a jaw could be so pretty

i had never seen a face so warm and comforting

it reminded me of the theory about the invisible string.

how we were connected before we had known

and how my heart was a priced possession you did
already own

i wrote poems and sonnets about your throaty laugh

so melodious and soulful, it could never be captured in
the stillness of a photograph

she's got these prettiest chestnut brown eyes

and if you look deeper into them

you'll see a desert with water pooling at the edge as she
cries

her eyes reflect a stranded desert, a place she was all
alone until she was all grown

she felt peace in being alone

for she had always been on her own.

she had never felt love or care

she had never known how to be soulfully bare

she wanted to feel not so lonely more times than some

she had never known how her lover, the one she dreamt
of more so than often would really come

but for her, he always would,

he had seen her desert and been her genie because he fell
in love with a beautiful goddess, he admitted it more
than the stars surrounding the moon could.

they say, always an angel, never a god

but she was one and so was he,

oh how they completed each other, it was a sight to see.

he saw the corner of her eyes crinkle every time she
smiled

he made it his mission to make her smile all the time
even if it meant crafting his hair wild.

she saw a golden heart in him with eyes as beautiful as
the sea

the sea that she had never seen

but watching his eyes made her feel as if she had never
looked at something so serene

she was his war.

his to fight, his to win over, and only his to adore.

he was her peace,

hers to rest upon, hers to calm in, and only hers to tease.

i crocheted your name on my heart

i wished for the yarns of your love to keep me together

only if i had been a little smart

only if i had known it was not the wool your were
twisting, it was also your promises of the false forever

i wondered if i could still hold on to the love we laced

or maybe it was all deception

oh how, deep down i knew the truth yet i chased you

how begrudgingly you made me hate my reflection

your name etched on all of my verses

and how you didn't care much, did you?

you rained me with all of these lies and crocheted
promises

but none it was ever true.

i am like a sunflower, patient and happy during the rain

and you're my sun, the one who lights me up and fills me with love so difficult to contain.

i am only living for the hope of it all

i've been hanging on for you like a star awaiting for the nightfall

i wonder how falling in love feels like

is it that thing your stomach does

or the kind of rush you feel on a bike

is it the thrumming in your heart

or how an aesthete views his art

is it the way you feel warmth blooming inside

or how your skin tingles every time you collide

it was 3am and i wrote a poetry

not caring if it was beautiful or ugly

i wrote about you

and your eyes; ah, mesmerizing ocean blue

i wrote about how i used to drowned in them

not knowing all you had wished was, for me to never
submerge again

you and i, we were never together

but just between us there was an unsaid promise of forever

we flirted and looked at each other for a beat too long

but i think both of us knew we would never be anything more than just a sad song

we were never meant to be engraved like tattoos

and yet you were never mine to lose

i loved you more than a friend

you knew but you liked to pretend

my love was never enough

but your love was always so rough

i think a part of me was glad that we wouldn't last

but another part of me never wanted you to be just another person from my past

watching at him, she wondered, "i hope i get to keep him forever"

his eyes betrayed hers before his empty promises of 'i would never' i used to think i wouldn't regret it all

and i would love you no matter what

but that was last fall

i now do regret how many hours and years

i wasted upon you

on someone who did nothing but fake promises but
never came through

i never should've accepted your gifts

because they're my favorite thing in the world and not
because of you,

they were my favorite long before you came along

but now they sit there on the table

and make me feel wrong

and now your pictures and calls and videos don't exist

and i count that as win

and i although may have deleted it all in haste

you were erased;

and all i know is that erasing you was not waste

dearest,

i've been betrayed before

i reasoned that my lover was the one

but i was double-crossed until i couldn't take it anymore

we were done before we had even begun.

those days and nights did not mean anyhow

and you waltz like a prince into my life

your promises made me believe as far as heartbreak
could allow

and one night you looked me in the eye, swore that
someday i would be your wife

i couldn't help but smile

the faith you had in me and us

but i wondered if it would fade in a while;

i chose to think it was not just lust but also love and
trust.

my love, as i write this on our wedding day

i know you're here to stay

and if we want to, someday we can run away.

longing to see you,

your sweetheart

my arms hold a moon

her closed eyes makes my heart swell

she's my snow even in june

his arms make me feel like home

his scent invades my senses

until i smell like his cologne

the picture of us was sadder than a funeral

but in that one moment we were happy,

we were magical.

if my heart is a black and white television

you add colors and beats to it.

we were destined for eternity

or so we thought

fate played its cards

and we lost

in English, you say 'I love you'

but in poetry we say, *'if my heart is a white sky,*

you're my artist, painting it pink, blue and orange.'

74

MOONLIT

MELANCHOLY

they want me to be as strong as a tiger

but i'm still a weakling trying be a fighter

my heart races everytime my mind overthinks

they want me to be as hearty as a dolphin

i'm exhausted of lying in their suffocating coffin

the pool in front my eyes is where my heart sinks

my jumbled mind doesn't stay calm

every moment of everyday that i'm out

feels like something's gonna harm

-     *an anxious girl who travels alone everyday*

i wept an ocean

until i was the one drowning in it

you get tired of it,

sick of dealing with shit,

same drill every single day,

so drained, don't know what to say.

at times you feel so alone

even people you know feel unknown

you feel so stuck

you just wanna give up.

they say it gets better one day

but it's not today.

you're back to square one

it's easier said than done.

day one, day two, day five

gradually you survive

day ten, day twenty, day thirty-two

it's actually getting better for you.

sadness doesn't keep you up anymore

it's not the same as it used to be before.

not all your days are bad

you're more happy than sad.

you work on you,

you'll get through.

im so tired of being the girl that i am

but the girl they want me to be is the one i know i never can

a people pleaser who loves herself too

dear nostalgic youth

where have you gone?

was i your ally,

or was i just a pawn?

when did i lose

those days of giggles and chuckles?

who stole the times

when we'd hop in the drizzling rain's puddles?

where are those parent-teacher meetings when

they complained about how chatty i used to be?

when did i stop going on amazing trips

when did my golden era turn into a sad reality?

i don't write much about people i loathe

so powerful, so full of rage, i'd swear on a blood oath.

for all i care they can go to hell

who's the angel, who's the devil, only time will tell

hate.

hate is a strong word.

at times, the lines between dislike

and hate are blurred.

that burning feeling in the chest,

gritting teeth and clenching fists.

fighting back those furious tears,

not only now but since years.

im just a girl

who wants to be the poetry

been writing for my own heart, hopelessly

like the never-ending galaxy for eternity

im just a girl

who wants to be cherished

with real feelings not just because we're destined

i think i will have everything that i've wished

i want to progress

but i'm too tired of the process

i keep screaming

but no one can hear it

i keep asking

but no one cares to help me

i keep silence

but im told i don't speak

i keep it all in

hiding it behind a forced grin

always the poet, never the poem

always a choice, never the one chosen

always the artist, never the art

always a bookgirl, never the girl in the book

always a verse, never the song

always a writer, never the one written for

always the one burning, never burnt for

always a giver, never the reciever

always a lover, never the one loved

always a pleaser, never the pleased one

always a reader, never the one read

maybe that's how my story goes

always weeping, but no tears for me would shed

if ghosts are real

then where did mine get lost?

was it angst or worry, my dear?

or did it drown in the cruel river of my past?

we're criticized for everything we say

what type of clothes we wear during the day

what color we dye our hair

or what type of products we use for skin care

we're questioned upon our taste in men

if they don't agree, we're frowned at even then

we're expected to obey them and shut our mouths all the time

even when they're committing a sinister crime

    -    *who are we?*

        we're only women.

when my folks head out

im left alone with a monster or two

i hear them argue and shout

its all shit about me and you

i wonder what i did to deserve this

been listening to shit since i was a little kid

why do people disguised as monsters even exist

im not afraid

it's all animosity

maybe one day i won't hesitate to lay out the truth

hushed cries echoed through my room

nobody saw and nobody heard

it was tucked away with the hollow sinking feeling in
my chest

i sobbed under the blanket until everything blurred.

she was a garden full of wildflowers

they swayed to the peaceful music

that was being played by the wind

she had this fragrance to her,

so sweet and yet spicy at the same time

and a kind of giggle you'd want to hear

she's the girl who writes poetries for her lover

the kind of girl who carries some heavy trauma from her
mother

she's the girl who feels abandoned by her dad

the kind of girl who wishes every night for her heart to
quit being sad

she's the girl who feels responsible about everything

the kind of girl who apologizes even for breathing

she's the kind of girl who gives away all her warmth

until she's a shuddering mess left between cold prickly
thorns

she's the kind of girl who loves deeply

but is always labelled as too needy.

she's the kind of girl who cries

always wanting peace but never reaches there

and yet she is the kind of girl who always tries

she gently said "i told you so"

but she never understood how much it meant to me and how it was everything and so much more

she never knew what he did for me

she never asked about it but hated him and wanted me to agree

she never saw how his eyes crinkled every time he found his favourite coffee being sipped by me

or how he got me these little orange flowers from his neighbour's garden, she never saw that, did she?

he hid his phone, she never saw that

i saw how his eyes had a hint of shame and how i went to her house just to find his favourite hat

i told her i broke up with that guy

she screamed "i told you so" but never asked me why

she never knew how i saw them kissing

she never knew how i lost a boyfriend and a best friend in one sitting

if the sun and the moon had a baby

it would be her

a paradox

she was the silent moonlight

faded midnight blue, calmer than the ocien view

she was the epitome of sunshine

glittery golden, somehow broken

i saw my friends running away from me

but we were only playing hide and seek

i was so naïve to actually see

how they had all laughed at me

it was sad how it turned out

friendships that i thought would be with me forever;
drowned.

my friends say im pretty

but why have i never felt as attractive as new york city

but i don't think they mean it as pretty in a 'you're as
gorgeous as the northern lights' way

i think they mean it as 'you're really cute'

and i appreciate it, you know

i've never had many people compliment me

so i take what i get

but sometimes it makes me sad

why am i never as beautiful as a sunset?

why the words that i deserve are, always left unsaid?

oh but you were just a teen

as sad as it may be you were hiding yet hoping to be
seen

how easily you felt like wanting to end your life

because death sounded better

than selling everyone with those same old lies

it's rather heartbreaking, how you starved yourself

hoping it would do you some help

the cuts on your arms weren't always unnoticed

or those scars from the blade marks on your wrist

you red-rimmed eyes stopped crinkling

and then your demons refrained them from twinkling

i've been told i shouldn't cry so much

even when i forbid them, i've been touched

i've been told i should paste a smile all the time

even when i feel nothing close to fine

i've been told i should lose weight

but they don't know how much being my own skin
makes me self hate

i've been told to gain a few pounds so i'd look more
lady-like

but what about those blood stained stripes i've marked
after midnights

i've been told to be stronger as if my emotional
vulnerability is a weakness

and they're the same people who mistake my politeness
for sweetness

i've been told that i laugh too loud

but what about those times when i had no one to pat my
back and say that they're proud

they say i have it easy

that i have it better

but im an only child

and even i have that gnawing pressure.

in the middle of the night

when i lie sleepless

all these thoughts of being alone

make me drown in hopelessness

it's no fun being by yourself

or how you become the parent when you're the eldest
child

or how invisible you become as the middle child

or how the youngest has been stereotyped by being
called the most spoilt

but for me, the grass is always greener on the other side

for i've never felt more alone that at home

or how i've longed to hug a sibling of my own.

a void in my chest that has felt vacant

every time i enter my house, after school or after college

the lack of a partner in crime, or a best friend from birth;

something i always acknowledge.

it's the feeling of knowing how heartbroken you are

but there's no shoulder to lean your head on or no one to
drive your around in the car.

it's as bad as watching your favourite book burn

and all you can do is watch, sob and yearn.

some people drift away

leaving memories in residue,

words you don't get to say,

and unexecuted plans you once brew

life feels empty sometimes

the sun goes up and my hope dies

the moon fades from the sky and im ready to survive

life feels merry

the blooming flowers seem like a garden planted by a fairy

the lake reflecting the water in all its glory

life feels like hell

the humans rotate around a carousel

and the dark grey sky changes to pastel

and so i entered into the night

my tattered white dress smeared of red stains

my manuscripts, faded like eclipse

my screams and pains

the tick,

      tick,

         tick,

            of my racing heart

my eyes streamed of crystal clear rains

all is fair in sadness and memories

loml (nishi's version)

i've had fights

i've had fun

i've caught sight of the prettiest shades of lights

i've had my eras of barbies, spinners and ribbons.

i've had nights where i cried

i've heard taylor swift and she helped me heal

i've learnt the contrast between self-respect and pride

i've never been the brainy one, i rely on how i feel.

i've sung along with loved ones at a concert

i've danced and enjoyed the moments i knew wouldn't
last

i've had phases of dresses and t-shirts

i've had years where i've failed and barely passed.

i've read a lot of romance

and it lead my standards up too high

real men now don't stand a chance

the worst part of reading is the good-bye.

i written words that reached my soul

verses that filled me whole

i've watched a lot of movies and shows

i've learnt a lesson or few

been ready for every hurdle life has thrown through

but you gotta play life, or it plays you.

this is just another advice

because this is the **letter of my life**

i woke up to another loss

a girl who was out late at night

now now, start with your questions

were her clothes too loose or too tight?

was her lively smile too bright?

did she giggle loudly or was it quiet?

did her eyes lose its shine when a man whistled at her in
the darkness of the moonlight?

did she shiver and start running in fright?

did she scream when you caught up?

did she cry for help while you crawled inside her like a
parasite?

did she feel like she was at a burial site?

was she left to die at the corner of a street at midnight?

did the guilt make him feel shame and disgust at his
mere sight?

could he clean up all that blood and her tries and
strangled cries with all her might?

she survived but her magical heart died that night.

i was only ten
i broke my arm bone
and i wondered if the pain would ever end
but it always had after then

i was only eleven
i had many friends, or so i thought, but don't we all?
friend is a crystal title, not everyone deserves to be
called
the world didn't end yet those betrayals never seem
small

i was only twelve
when i was heartbroken over a silly boy
and i believed that my world would end
how i wish i knew it hadn't, would i have avoided
feeling overwhelmed?

i was only thirteen
when i was concious about how i looked
i was convinced everything was wrong with me
my world didn't end but i was drowning in a self-
loathing sea

i was only fourteen
when i was heartbroken again, not by a boy but a man-
child
how i wish i could erase it all but i know i wouldn't
if i hadn't felt that pain i wouldn't be as strong and as
wild

i was only fifteen
when i fell in love again, desperate for some
companionship
oh how i lost a piece of my soul, writing, the one that
made me whole
love made you stronger, i had read, and yet it made me
weaker than i had ever felt

i was only sixteen
worrying about everything
oh how i was flying in love while he was not
i gave away pieces of me until i was as vacant as satan's
heart

i was only seventeen
when my heart was feeling like a garden of flowers
a delicate flower that was being ripped, petal-by-petal
but my world didn't end when i accepted the empty
vows

i was only eighteen
when i broke hearts – not only my own
how i wish i wouldn't feel guilty for choosing myself
over them
just when i thought i wouldn't be okay, girlhood saved
me by being a gem

i was almost nineteen
when i wanted to hurt myself only to numb the pain
how confusing to feel like wanting to live a long life not
in vain
and yet wanting to drown in some pain because
numbness is worse to chain

even when i had been chastised
loved and laughed and lost plenty in this life
and yet,
long story short, i survived.

i feel broken hearts as if they're my own

i understand the spiral of being alone

i wish i had powers to make you feel loved

and magic to heal

but i see through everything you try to conceal

i see the marks on your wrists,

bags under your eyes,

i know the sadness behind your goodbyes

maybe my tortured words speak with you

and give you comfort

i hope it heals all the agonizing hurt

i know it feels like the end of the world right now

but soon you'll get better

i wish you happy days and peaceful nights through this
letter

114

ABOUT THE AUTHOR

Nishi is just a girl, living in Mumbai, India. She is an undergrad studying English Lit.

While pursuing her studies, Nishi channels her creativity into the realm of poetry, where she finds solace and self-expression. As someone who often struggles to articulate her thoughts verbally, poetry serves as a powerful outlet for her emotions.

Poetry, for her, is not just an art form but a means of healing—a way to make sense of the world and find peace amidst the chaos.

Apart from writing, she is an annoyingly fast reader and she enjoys watching TV shows and listening to Taylor Swift and she loves making playlists.

To contact her:

Instagram - www.instagram.com/authornishi

E-mail – authornishi@gmail.com

www.ingramcontent.com/pod-product-compliance
Lightning Source LLC
Chambersburg PA
CBHW021555150726
47990CB00006B/2555